Love Knows No Limit...

Elisabeth Elliot

D0551015

Pickering & Inglis, Ltd.
London

Love Knows No Limit . . .

First appeared in Christian Herald *magazine.*

First published in this format in 1982 by
Good News Publishers,
9825 West Roosevelt Road,
Westchester, Illinois 60153.

Published in England by
Pickering & Inglis, Ltd., London.

First printing July 1982.

Cover photo: Robert Cushman Hayes

Good News Publishers ISBN 0-89107-270-5
Pickering & Inglis ISBN 0-7208-0624-0

Love Knows No Limit...

It is early morning. I lie as usual in a double bed, and as usual I wake and give thanks for the sleep and safety of the night, for health and warmth and food and friends, for work to do and strength to do it. There is, as before, a layer of silence above the distant sound of traffic.

There are some other sounds as well, not usual at all. Instead of the sharp, peremptory bark of MacDuff I hear the muted and mournful howl of Johnny Reb, a beagle who belongs to the next-door neighbors. The garbage truck grinds up the hill outside my window (for this house is on a hill). And there is the sound of someone breathing—beside me.

Lord, Father of Spirits, Lover of Souls, my Light and my Stronghold, thanks! Thanks for the greatest of earthly blessings, marriage.

My prayer goes on for a little while—thanksgiving and petition (that I may be the sort of wife I ought to be, that together we may accomplish the will of the Father). Later, in the kitchen while I fix breakfast, I think about this business of being transplanted. We have a nice little brick house on a very quiet street with a view of the Atlanta skyline from the kitchen windows.

Usually to get married means to be

transplanted. Always it means to hand over power. Our Lord has a sense of humor, and he has heard me over the past couple of years as I went around talking about marriage, "popping off" about how a woman is supposed to behave toward a man. He has "read" my book, too, I'm sure—*Let Me Be a Woman*. He knows, too, that I believed every word of it, believed it was the truth of God that I spoke.

"All right," He said, "try it again."

He gave me a third husband four and a half years after the death of the second, and He said, "Did you really believe all those things you said and wrote? Have another go at it to make sure."

Love means self-giving. Self-giving means sacrifice. Sacrifice means death. Those are some of the things I've said. I got them out of the same Book, the only thoroughly and eternally reliable Sourcebook. The principles of gain through loss, of joy through sorrow, of getting by giving, of fulfillment by laying down, of life out of death is what that Book teaches, and the people who have believed it enough to live it out in simple, humble, day-by-day practice are people who have found the gain, the joy, the getting, the fulfillment, the life. I really do believe that.

"Lord," I ask, "help me to live it out."

"All right," He says to me, "here's your chance."

In Georgia.

Georgia, where I'm the one with the accent. They call me "Lizbeth." They "carry" children to school or friends to the airport, they don't "take" them. Photographers "make" rather than "take" pictures. They drink "Co-Cola," they go to "fillin' stations," they eat "congealed" salads, and words like *spin* and *hill* have two long drawn-out syllables.

Sometimes we can trace strange connections in the patterns God works in human lives. One of the last things my late husband Add Leitch said to me was that if God should restore him to health he would like to become a hospital chaplain. My new husband is a hospital chaplain.

He took me to Milledgeville to visit the women in the geriatric ward.

"How ya doin', Miz Jackson?"

"Tol'ble well, tol'ble well, preacher. Come here, Ah'm'on' pray for you."

She rises, slowly and painfully, from her chair, places her hands on his shoulders, and repeats with deep fervor the whole of the Lord's prayer.

A woman with beautiful white hair sits in a wheelchair that is hung with more than a dozen pouches, purses and drawstring bags. She quotes from Chaucer's *Canterbury Tales,* talks knowledgeably of Canterbury Cathedral, of Henry VIII, and Cranmer's Prayer Book, winking at me as she talks, as though the two of us are privy to something Lars doesn't know.

We eat breakfast with Mr. Smith, a very handsome man with white hair, ruddy skin, and bright blue eyes. He is wearing a blue shirt and blue sweater. He tells us a story which brings into sharp focus the words of the wedding vows—"in sickness and in health, for better, for worse." His wife has been a patient at Milledgeville for three years.

"When she first got sick I carried her everywhere. I did. The doctor said, 'She'll get worse, every week and every month. So if you want to go on any trips or anywhere, go now.' We had some good times, me and her.

But the doctor said, 'You cain't stand it. You won't be able to stand it.' Well, I said, 'Ah'm'on' hang on long's I can.'

"I took care of her for five years, but I lost fifty-two pounds just from worry. I was so tense they broke three needles tryin' to put a shot in my arm. Well, I carried her to twenty-five doctors, but they couldn't do nothin'. It's brain deter'ation, they told me. I did everything for her. I dressed her and fed her and everything, but it like to whup me and if it hadn't of been for the good Lord I'da never made it. Doctor said, 'I'da sworn you'd never last six months.' But a lot of people were prayin' for me. Oh yes. But finally I had to give up and put her here.

"She cain't do nothin'. Cain't move or speak or hear. She's in the prebirth position, legs and arms locked, heels locked up tight behind. You cain't straighten her out. But I come every other day. I go in and kiss her 'bout a dozen times, jes' love her to death. I talk to her. She don't hear, but she knows my touch.

"Well." Mr. Smith finished his story. "I work for the florist here. Volunteer work, you know. I go around the wards, carrying flowers."

We went later to see Mrs. Smith. If ever there was a sight to confound a man's love for a woman, to strain to the breaking point the most potent human passion, we saw it in that stark white crib—a crumpled scrap of inert humanity. But there is a love that is strong as death, a love many waters cannot quench, floods cannot drown.

I thought of that kind of love not long afterwards, and I thought of it with shame, for I had been disturbed by a petty thing. It is sweet Georgia springtime now, lavish compensation for January's cold, and the birds sing. But I, being still a sinner, can be disturbed by a petty thing. Back I went to the Sourcebook, to the thirteenth chapter of 1 Corinthians, for a clear description of how I ought to act if I really wanted my prayer answered ("Make me the sort of wife I ought to be").

What I found was the precise opposite of my own inclinations in this instance, because this time I was quite sure that my husband was wrong. Reading my own name in place of the word *love,* followed by the opposites of each characteristic described, I saw my own face in the glass and the truth knocked me down. "E. loses patience, is destructive, possessive, anxious to impress, cherishes inflated ideas of her own importance, has bad manners, pursues selfish advantage, is touchy, keeps account of evil. . . ."

I couldn't go on. The antidote to these horrors was love—the kind that "knows no limit to its endurance, no end to its trust, no fading of its hope; it can outlast anything. It is, in fact, the one thing that still stands when all else has fallen."

The Word of God is light, and in its light we see light. My perspective changed; I saw what had bothered me as a petty thing, as nothing. Peace and equilibrium were restored—and that without a "sharing" session. "Thy words were found and I did eat them, and they were unto me the joy and rejoicing of my heart." "Thy statutes have been my songs in the house of my pilgrimage" (Ps. 119:54). Thanks be to God for such songs.